Spotlight on Songwriters

BILLIE EILISH

Ursula Pang

CREATED BY Humans

Published in 2027 by The Rosen Publishing Group, Inc.
2544 Clinton Street, Buffalo, NY 14224

First edition

Editor: Greg Roza
Designer: Michael Flynn

Photo Credits: Cover DFree/Shutterstock.com; (series background) Yuliya Chsherbakova/Shutterstock.com; p. 5 Andie Mills/Alamy; p. 7 Daniel DeSlover/ZUMA Wire/Alamy; p. 9 imageSPACE/MediaPunch/Alamy; p. 11 Giulia Manfieri/Alamy; p. 13 (main) Christian Bertrand/Shutterstock.com; p. 13 (inset) bella1105/Shutterstock.com; p. 15 McSleepy/Shutterstock.com; p. 17 Featureflash Photo Agency/Shutterstock.com; p. 19 AFF/Alamy Live News; p. 21 Ben Houdijk/Shutterstock.com.

Cataloging-in-Publication Data

Names: Pang, Ursula.
Title: Billie Eilish / Ursula Pang.
Description: Buffalo, New York : Created by Humans, an imprint of Rosen Publishing, 2027. | Series: Spotlight on songwriters| Includes glossary and index.
Identifiers: ISBN 9781534553378 (pbk.) | ISBN 9781534553385 (library bound) | ISBN 9781534553392 (ebook)
Subjects: LCSH: Eilish, Billie, 2001---Juvenile literature. | Singers--United States--Biography--Juvenile literature.
Classification: LCC ML3930.E35 P36 2027 | DDC 782.42164092--dc23

Manufactured in the United States of America

CONTENTS

GROWING UP 4
"OCEAN EYES" 6
FIRST ALBUM 8
BILLBOARD SUPERSTAR 10
AWARD WINNER 12
RISING FAME 14
TOP OF HER GAME 16
IN THE MOVIES 18
CARING SONGWRITER 20
GLOSSARY 22
FOR MORE INFORMATION 23
INDEX 24

Growing Up

Billie Eilish Pirate Baird O'Connell was born on December 18, 2001. She grew up in Los Angeles, California. Her parents **homeschooled** Billie and her older brother Finneas. Billie's mom, Maggie Baird, is a famous actor. She helped Billie and Finneas to become musicians.

"Ocean Eyes"

In 2015, when Billie was just 13 years old, her brother asked her to sing a song he had written for his band. Together they recorded the song "Ocean Eyes." They put the song online for people to hear and it quickly became very **popular**!

First Album

Billie signed with a record company when she was 14. One year later, she released an eight-song album titled *Don't Smile at Me*. Billie and Finneas wrote the album, and it was a big hit with fans. Billie's popularity was about to skyrocket!

Billboard Superstar

In 2019, Billie put out her first full-length album—*When We Fall Asleep, Where Do We Go?* This album rose to number one on the **Billboard** 200 chart. The song "Bad Guy" rose to number one on the Billboard 100 chart! Billie was more popular than ever.

Award Winner

In 2020, *When We Fall Asleep, Where Do We Go?* won four **Grammy Awards**. Billie became the youngest artist to win the four big Grammys: Best New Artist, Album of the Year, Record of the Year, and Song of the Year. What an honor for such a young songwriter!

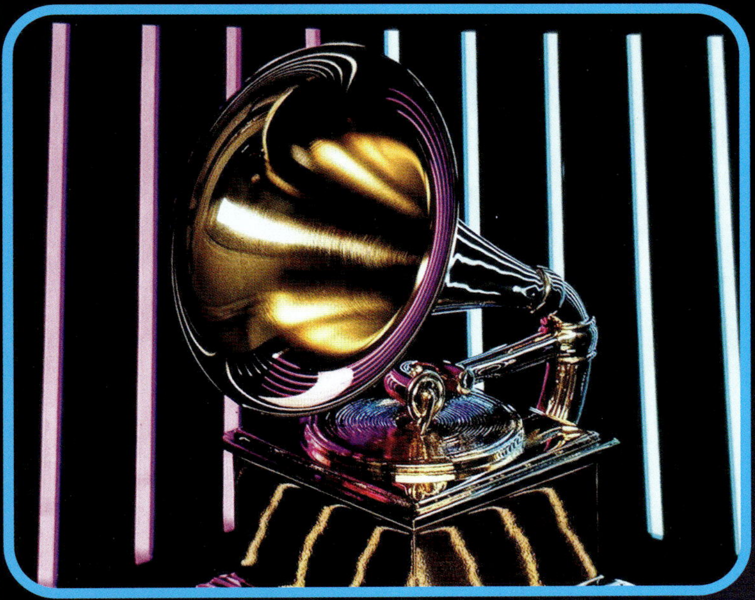

WHEN WE ALL FALL ASLEEP

Rising Fame

Billie won another Grammy in 2021 for the song "Everything I Wanted." She also released her second album that year, *Happier Than Ever*. The songs on this album explore Billie's personal feelings. It was another huge hit with fans all over the world.

Happier
Than Ever
Switch to video
Happier Than Ever
E Billie Eilish
0:11
4:58

Top of Her Game

In 2024, Billie released her third album, *Hit Me Hard and Soft*. The song "Wildflower" from this album won the Grammy for Song of the Year in 2026. In 2025, the video game *Fortnite* added Billie's clothing style as an outfit players can unlock.

In the Movies

In 2022, Billie wrote the song "No Time to Die" for a movie with the same name. She won an **Academy Award** for it! Also that year, Billie and Finneas wrote songs for the movie *Barbie*. The song "What Was I Made For?" won two Grammys and another Academy Award.

Caring Songwriter

Billie Eilish speaks out about topics many other young people care about. These topics include bullying, women's rights, and the **environment**. She has become an important voice for the youth of the world. Billie will continue to explore these ideas in her songwriting career!

GLOSSARY

Academy Awards: Prizes given every year in the United States for the people who create movies.

Billboard: Weekly lists created by the U.S. magazine *Billboard* that rank popular music.

environment: The natural world around us.

Grammy Awards: Prizes given every year in the United States for the people who create music.

homeschool: To teach one's children in the home, rather than in a public or private school.

popular: Liked by many people.

FOR MORE INFORMATION

BOOKS

Holmes, Kristy. *Music*. St. Paul, MN: North Star Editions, 2025.

Nguyen, Suzane. *Billie Eilish*. Bloomington, MN: Torque, 2025

WEBSITES

Billie Eilish
www.imdb.com/name/nm8483808
Learn more about Billie's many songwriting accomplishments here.

Billie Eilish Facts for Kids
kids.kiddle.co/Billie_Eilish
Read more about Billie's life and career at this website.

Publisher's note to educators and parents: Our editors have carefully reviewed these websites to ensure that they are suitable for students. Many websites change frequently, however, and we cannot guarantee that a site's future contents will continue to meet our high standards of quality and educational value. Be advised that students should be closely supervised whenever they access the internet.

INDEX

A
Academy Award, 18

B
"Bad Guy," 10
Baird, Maggie, 4
Barbie, 18
Billboard charts, 10

D
"Don't Smile at Me," 8

E
"Everything I Wanted," 14

F
Finneas, 4, 6, 8, 18
Fortnite, 16

G
Grammy Awards, 12, 14, 16, 18

H
Happier Than Ever, 14
Hit Me Hard and Soft, 16

L
Los Angeles, California, 4

N
"No Time to Die," 18

O
"Ocean Eyes," 6

W
"What Was I Made For?," 18
"Wildflowers," 16